GERMAN CAPITAL SHIPS

Leipzig under tow, possibly after an incident with British submarine *Sealion* in December 1939. She was later nearly sunk by a Soviet submarine in the Baltic! (MN/1578/25).

PAUL BEAVER
GERMAN CAPITAL SHIPS

WORLD WAR 2 PHOTO ALBUM NUMBER 14

A selection of German wartime photographs
from the Bundesarchiv, Koblenz

PSL Patrick Stephens, Cambridge

First published in 1980

British Library Cataloguing in Publication Data

German capital ships.—(World War 2 photo albums; 14).
 1. Germany—Kriegsmarine
 2. Warships—History—20th century—Pictorial works
 I. Title II. Beaver, Paul III. Series 623.
  82'52'0943   VA513

ISBN 0 85059 395 6 (Casebound)
ISBN 0 85059 396 4 (Softbound)

Photoset in 10pt Plantin Roman. Printed in Great Britain on 100gsm Pedigree coated cartridge and bound by The Garden City Press Limited, Letchworth, Hertfordshire SG6 1JS, for the publishers, Patrick Stephens Limited, Bar Hill, Cambridge, CB3 8EL, England.

CONTENTS

Acknowledgements
The author and publisher would like to express their sincere thanks to Frau Marianne Loenartz of the Bundesarchiv for her assistance, without which this book would have been impossible.

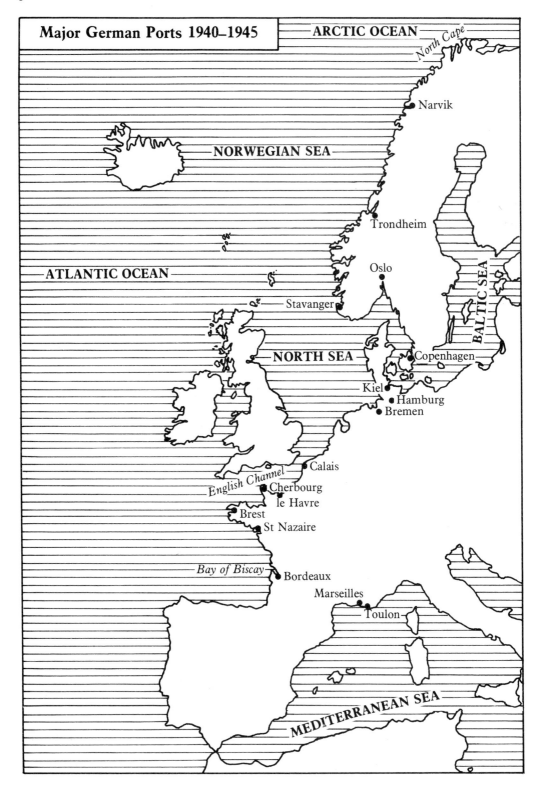

Major German Ports 1940–1945

ARCTIC OCEAN

North Cape

● Narvik

NORWEGIAN SEA

● Trondheim

ATLANTIC OCEAN

Oslo ●

Stavanger ●

BALTIC SEA

NORTH SEA

● Copenhagen

Kiel ●

● Hamburg
● Bremen

● Calais

English Channel ● Cherbourg
● le Havre

Brest ●
● St Nazaire

Bay of Biscay ● Bordeaux

Marseilles ●
● Toulon

MEDITERRANEAN SEA

The German Navy, or Kriegsmarine as it was called between 1935 and 1945, possessed on paper in 1939 some of the best major surface units of any navy in the world. With hindsight, we can now see that the mere possession of these vessels, threatening as they were, did mean that they would be decisive in any clash with the Allies. Unfortunately for the Kriegsmarine and its chief, Gross-Admiral Raeder, they were not fully tried in action because of the interference of politicians and a clash of personalities.

In 1919, the Treaty of Versailles set limits on the old Kaiserliche Marine. These limits were designed to prevent Germany from again challenging the victors of the 1914–18 conflict. Germany was not, however, a party to the Washington Naval Treaty which limited the major powers' size of warship, and by the early 1930s she was transgressing the restrictive clauses of the Versailles document. Two years after Hitler came to power Germany repudiated the Treaty of Versailles, on March 16 1935, and into the open came the whole naval building programme.

In 1939, the Kriegsmarine was committed to a trade war with the United Kingdom, her allies and Empire. The German Naval Staff, headed by Raeder, had advocated the Z-plan which would give Germany the warships successfully to challenge the Royal Navy by 1944/45.

On April 27 1939, Hitler repudiated the Anglo-German Naval Treaties of 1935/37 and the German Fleet began deploying for an offensive operation against British merchantmen. The trade or commerce raiders usually operated alone and had a devastating effect on independently sailing merchant ships. The Royal Navy's convoy system had not moved into top gear and, although Hitler gave the U-boat arm first priority for men and supplies, armoured ships (or *panzer-schiffs*) such as the *Admiral Graf Spee* and the

Deutschland wrought havoc in distant sea areas such as the South Atlantic. Both these vessels used every weight-saving measure possible, such as welded construction and triple turrets, to stay within the Terms of Versailles. Hence their name, conjured up by the British Press, of Pocket Battleships.

The *Graf Spee* was caught off the Plate Estuary in December 1939 by Commodore Harwood's Cruiser squadron after a merry dance around the South Atlantic. She was scuttled off Montevideo on December 17 1939, the first major blow to the prestige of the Kriegsmarine. The *Deutschland* had her name changed to *Lützow* in 1940, and served the war as we shall see below.

Meanwhile, in the North Atlantic, the sister-ships *Gneisenau* and *Scharnhorst* were raiding the convoy routes, hoping to punch a hole in the Northern Patrol of the Royal Navy. This patrol was designed as a blockade of German sea routes and was operated by cruisers and armed merchant cruisers (AMCs). In one of these confrontations the AMC *Rawalpindi* was sunk in the Denmark Strait, but not before her convoy had escaped. A similar fate overtook the *Jervis Bay*, an east-bound convoy's only escort. Again the convoy (HX84) scattered and the heroic action of the *Jervis Bay* saved them from a big ship's guns – in this case *Admiral Scheer*.

In May 1940, during the Norwegian Campaign, the old aircraft carrier HMS *Glorious* was returning from the battle area with RAF and RN aircraft embarked. She and her close escort of two destroyers were swamped when the 'deadly duo' appeared over the horizon on June 8 1940. Although the destroyers flung themselves at the German battlecruisers, the 18,600-ton carrier and her cargo of aircraft went to the bottom, but HMS *Acasta* did manage to hit *Scharnhorst* with a torpedo and the latter had to limp into Trondheim for repairs. While there she was attacked by RN Skua aircraft and later at sea by Swordfish, all to no avail.

It would perhaps be relevant to take a look at these two battlecruisers of revolutionary design. In 1933, after Hitler's rise to power, the German Navy set about systematically rebuilding its forces which had been depleted by the Treaty of Versailles. The *Scharnhorst* of 31,800 tons was a fast battlecruiser, with good protection, nine 28 cm guns and with her sister-ship

Gneisenau presented a serious threat to the Atlantic shipping lanes. They were graceful warships, with, after refits, clipper stems and long fo'c's'les. With a turn of speed of some 32 knots they could outrun anything they could not overwhelm, except perhaps HMS *Hood* – although this meeting never took place!

Perhaps the most famous German warship of World War 2 was the 50,153-ton KM *Bismarck*. She was launched with great ceremony on February 14 1939, and carried eight 38 cm guns and 6×2 15 cm secondary batteries, plus six Arado Ar 196 seaplanes which were launched by catapult for spotting and general reconnaissance. Her sister-ship *Tirpitz* carried a larger complement and differed slightly from *Bismarck*, probably as a result of the experience gained in fitting out the latter on the River Elbe. One of the differences was the addition of anti-surface vessel torpedo-tubes to the *Tirpitz* – rather strange for a battleship.

The *Bismarck*'s sea-going career was not exactly spectacular, but her fame stems from the largest running fight in the annals of modern naval history – Operation Rheinübung. Raeder planned to send a powerful squadron to raid the important transatlantic convoy tracks and to take the place of the fast battlecruiser squadron which had reached the safety of the Brest by this time. The Oberkommando der Marine (OKM) or German Admiralty had laid on seven support and supply ships in mid-Atlantic (including *Esso Hamburg*). The commissioning ceremony in mid-1940 was followed by a series of trials and shakedowns in the Baltic. The flag officer for the *Bismarck* cruise was Admiral Lütjens who wore his flag in the battleship; the other warship in the squadron was the heavy cruiser *Prinz Eugen*. The RAF kept a constant watch on the pair after they left Gdynia in mid-May. May 20 saw them at Christiansand and London informed courtesy of the brave Norwegian underground. The Home Fleet was alerted and *Hood* and *Prince of Wales*, plus two 'County' Class cruisers, sailed for the sealanes off Greenland – the expected track of the Axis ships on their way to the Atlantic. A photo-reconnaissance Spitfire identified the squadron in Norwegian waters before the weather ruled out further airborne reconnaissance. By this time, *King George V*, *Repulse* and *Victorious* were at sea off Iceland closing another route to the Ocean.

On May 23 the *Suffolk* sighted the squadron in the Denmark Strait and the *Hood* and the new battleship *Prince of Wales* were vectored in for the kill. The resultant engagement stunned the Royal Navy to a man – 95 officers and 1,321 men perished in the icy water off Iceland when the *Hood* blew up! The *Prince of Wales* was also damaged so severely that she was forced to break off the engagement and run to harbour. *Bismarck*, for her part, had been hit and was losing precious fuel oil.

Victorious later launched an air strike, and some advantage was gained when a hit was scored, slowing the battleship (or Schlachtschiff) down. *Prinz Eugen* was detached to Brest at this and *Bismarck* proceeded indirectly towards a Biscay port, with the RN out of touch. At this stage the United States became involved when, some 24 hours after a hasty German signal, the battleship was spotted by a PBY Catalina flying-boat of the RAF, flown by an Anglo-American crew led by a naval pilot from Missouri. This position was immediately flashed to Admiralty Intelligence enabling *Ark Royal* to launch her Swordfish aircraft. Damage was inflicted during this attack causing *Bismarck* to head into the waiting guns of *Rodney* and KGV. The 4th Destroyer Flotilla and *Dorsetshire* sealed her fate with torpedoes. It had taken a large fleet of seven battleships, 12 cruisers, two carriers and five destroyers to track and destroy this battleship in the relatively confined waters off the European Coast. Had the squadron escaped into the ocean, the hunt in mid-Atlantic does not bear thinking about at a time when Britain was standing alone. *Prinz Eugen*, which lived to fight another day, was finally expended as an atom bomb target in November 1947.

Previously, early in 1941, *Scharnhorst* and *Gneisenau* had made a successful cruise around the Halifax convoy routes in Operation Berlin, and managed to sink 22 merchantmen, including 16 in one action, escaping the attentions of three RN battleships which searched for them. However, when they returned to the occupied French naval base of Brest, on March 22 1941, they were refitted in company with the heavy cruiser *Prinz Eugen*. After initial photo-reconnaissance, the Royal Air Force's Bomber Command and the United States Army Air Force paid regular visits by night and day respectively. Precautions at sea against another raiding breakout included the stationing of Allied submarines off Brest for several months.

One of the worst defeats for Britain in 1942, in terms of material damage and loss of morale, was the famous Channel Dash (Operation Cerberus), by the battlecruisers *Gneisenau* and *Scharnhorst* and the heavy cruiser *Prinz Eugen*. These three Capital ships had been refitted and repaired at Brest between March 1941 and January 1942, but as Allied bombers visited them regularly, the High Command in Berlin was anxious that serious damage might be caused, making them unseaworthy again.

The Naval Staff, led by Gross-Admiral Erich Raeder, however, held the view that if these units remained on the French Atlantic coast they would prove a definite threat to the Royal Navy in the important convoy routes of the Western Atlantic and Southwestern Approaches. Raeder argued that if *Tirpitz* was operational in northern waters threatening Allied convoys to Russia, then the Home Fleet would find the task of covering Norway and France nigh impossible. Hitler appears to have given Raeder the choice of dismantling the Brest squadron and using their heavy armament on the Russian Front, or of despatching them around the heavily guarded British waters to Germany. Naturally, Raeder jumped for the latter choice, although he would have preferred a voyage around Scotland, through the Faroes–Iceland Gap. The flag officer-in-charge of the operation was to be the Commander Battleships, Vize-Admiral Cilax and he, surprisingly, supported Hitler's view that a Channel Dash would be so unexpected as to be successful.

Considerable thought and planning went into this unprecedented move, both on the German side and by Naval Intelligence in London. Such items as the state of the tide, the phase of the moon and the state of the swept channels through the defensive minefields had to be considered. The Kriegsmarine employed eight minesweeper flotillas to clear the way through the numerous minefields off the French coast.

The Royal Navy and the Royal Air Force took all the precautions that were possible in their operational readiness state. However, when the time came for the actual operation, the British were plagued by a whole series of operational problems and chain of unfortunate events. The German squadron, which left Brest on the night of February 11 1942, managed to slip past the blockade submarine *Sealion* and the fighter sweeps put up during the next day failed to notice anything which they considered unusual for 11 hours! It was only when the squadron had reached Cap Griz Nez, some 260 miles (666 km) up Channel, that full-scale destroyer and aircraft attacks were launched, including the courageous Swordfish sortie led by Lieutenant Commander Eugene Esmonde, DSO, for which he was awarded a posthumous Victoria Cross.

The Kriegsmarine did not have it all its own way because *Scharnhorst* struck a mine sown by Bomber Command during the last few days, followed by both battlecruisers striking magnetic mines. *Gneisenau* and *Prinz Eugen* managed to reach the safe haven of Brunsbuttel without further incident. Although the *Scharnhorst* reached Wilhelmshaven on February 13, she was quite badly damaged and was out of action for some time. *Gneisenau* now received a visit by Allied bombers which effectively put her out of action at Kiel until July 1942.

In early 1943, *Scharnhorst* was ready for action again and after two unsuccessful passages, the first on January 11 with *Prinz Eugen* , she reached Norway to join *Tirpitz* and *Lützow* (ex-*Deutschland*) on March 8. The massing of these heavy German surface units in Norwegian waters actually meant that the Allies stopped their Russian convoys for the summer of 1943, thus relieving some of the pressure on the Eastern Front. September 22 1943 saw the famous midget submarine attack on Altenfjord when *Tirpitz* was hit and disabled but the other two warships were untouched. *Lützow* soon departed for the Fatherland for a major refit leaving *Scharnhorst* the only operational capital ship to threaten the Russian convoys.

In the middle of December 1943, the Admiralty in London had deciphered sufficient signals from the Admiral Northern Waters (Narvik) to the Admiral Battlegroup (Altenfjord), to allow Admiral Fraser in HMS *Duke of York* in company with the cruisers *Jamaica* and *Belfast* to close with the *Scharnhorst* (Käpitan zur See Hintze), which was out convoy hunting. Because of bad weather, the battlecruiser had lost touch with her screen of five destroyers of the 4th Flotilla and, in the early morning of December 26 1943, the Battle of the North Cape was fought. Only 36 men survived from the proud battlecruiser KM *Scharnhorst*, which sank with the whole staff of Konter-Admiral Bey as well as the regular ship's company.

This left *Tirpitz* in northern waters, and despite repeated torpedo and bomb attacks by the combined might of six RN carriers including *Victorious* and *Furious*, she was still afloat. Their gallant attacks only gave the strategic situation a three-month respite and it eventually took a raid of 32 Lancaster bombers, armed with special bombs, to turn the *Tirpitz* into a capsized wreck at Tromsö on November 12 1944. The last operational German battleship had been put out of action and in fact she was scrapped *in situ* in 1948.

The career of the *Tirpitz*, the largest German battleship, must be considered to be a very negative one, especially if one realises that the closest she came to an Allied surface vessel was to *Ijora*, a Russian merchantman from QP8 which had been attacked by the screen destroyer *Friedrich Ibn* on March 8 1942. How different history might have been if this great 'floating battery' had been allowed to have been the tool of the experienced naval staff in Berlin instead of a dictator's toy.

Turning our attention now to the heavy cruisers, we have already touched on the careers of several. When World War 2 started the German shipyards had launched five units, the earliest being *Admiral Hipper* in February 1937. This shows just how late the Kriegsmarine was in the design field, but they had the advantage of modern technology; the disadvantage was, of course, that only a couple were in commission by the outbreak of hostilities.

Hipper first came into action, it seems, during Operation Nordmark in February 1940 when in company with *Scharnhorst* and *Gneisenau* and attendant destroyers, she unsuccessfully tried to hinder the UK–Scandinavia convoys. On April 8 1940 after losing contact with a minelaying force, HMS *Glowworm* was caught and sunk by *Hipper* after first valiantly attacking and ramming the heavy cruiser. The Germans were now engaged in occupying Norway and *Hipper*, under the command of Kapitän zur See Heye, was allocated to the Trondheim Group. In mid-April *Hipper* escaped the clutches of the *Warspite* force and rendezvoused off Stavanger with the two battlecruisers. In June the heavy cruiser was again in action, this time against the forces evacuating from Norway. The sinking of HMS *Glorious* by

the *Hipper*'s companions has been touched on previously.

The battlegroup continued northwards beyond the Arctic Circle but did not sight another target. Returning via the Iceland–Faeroes gap, *Gneisenau* was hit by a torpedo and the group split its forces leaving *Admiral Hipper* to spend the rest of the summer unsuccessfully raiding merchant traffic in the Arctic, before she returned to Kiel.

In September she made another abortive attempt at raiding but returned to Kiel after only six days at sea. In December, she at last managed to break through into the Atlantic under the command of Kapitän zur See Meisel. The ship encountered convoy WS5A and briefly exchanged fire with HMS *Berwick* before running for Brest where she berthed on December 27 1940.

Hipper departed Brest on February 1 1941 to continue her Atlantic raiding and succeeded in sinking seven out of nine unescorted merchantmen from convoy SLS64 before arriving at Brest on February 15. In March 1941, the *Hipper* made a dash for Kiel, but chose the northabout route through the Denmark Strait, and arrived safely on March 28. A year later, she was again in Norwegian waters with her destroyers at Trondheim ready for Arctic operations in the summer of that year. She was now part of Admiral Schniewind's Force 1 and in company with *Tirpitz* was stationed at Altenfjord to prey on the Russian convoys and carry out offensive mining operations. Later in the year her commander was replaced by Kapitän zur See Hartmann and she was again active against the Arctic convoys.

On the last day of 1942, *Hipper* was hit whilst attacking convoy JW51B with *Lützow*. It was not until March 1945 that the cruiser was again on any active service. This phase of her life was not a happy one as she was mainly engaged in covering the evacuation of East Prussia and Danzig—the greatest evacuation in history. In April, *Hipper* was badly damaged by RAF bombers at Kiel and less than a month later she was scuttled in Heikendorfer Bight.

Her sister-ship *Blücher*, on the other hand, had a very short career: she was launched in June 1937 and was sunk whilst forcing her way up Oslofjord on April 9 1940. Her Norwegian operations were under the direction of Konter-Admiral Kunmetz and her group included *Lützow* and *Emden*.

Generally similar to the *Hipper* Class, the *Prinz Eugen* Class had the classic cruiser clipper bow. The name-ship of the class, *Prinz Eugen,* was the last heavy cruiser to be completed for the Kriegsmarine although both her sister-ships were launched in the next year, 1939. *Lützow* (not to be confused with the armoured ship *Deutschland,* whose name was changed to the former in 1940), was sold incomplete to the Reich's then ally, Soviet Russia, in 1940. The Russians were unable to complete her by May 1941 and whilst in Leningrad she was bombed by the Luftwaffe in April 1942. Renamed *Tallin* later that year she served as an artillery battery against the soldiers of the country of her birth. In 1944 she was renamed *Petropavlovsk* and was scrapped in 1950.

The third member of the class was the *Seydlitz.* She was converted into an aircraft carrier in 1942, but by April 1945, as she was still not complete, she was scuttled. The Russians, on capturing Königsberg where she lay, refloated and renamed her *Poltava,* but by 1950 as completion was still not in sight she, like her sister-ship *Petropavlovsk,* was scrapped.

KM *Prinz Eugen,* famed for her part in the *Bismarck* operation and the Channel Dash, did not always have things her own way. On the night of July 1–2 1940, German capital ships were attacked by the RAF at Kiel, the *Prinz Eugen* being hit twice but not seriously damaged. During her move to Norway with *Admiral Scheer,* she was again attacked by a bomber, but this time, February 22 1942, the attacking aircraft was shot down. Just off Trondheim, however, the RN submarine *Trident* was waiting to attack the force, *Prinz Eugen* was hit at the stern and had to return to Germany to effect repairs. She was replaced by the *Lützow* moving northwards to Trondheim. In January 1943, the *Prinz Eugen* again moved north, and on this occasion the submarine and air attacks against her and *Scharnhorst* were unsuccessful. August 1944 saw *Prinz Eugen* deployed against Soviet troops in the Gulf of Riga area and these operations continued into April 1945 when she was again in company with *Lützow.*

On May 9, *Prinz Eugen* in company now with the light cruiser *Nürnberg* surrendered at Copenhagen. She was transferred to the US Navy and expended as a target for atomic tests in the Pacific in November 1947. A sad end to Germany's most successful cruiser of World War 2.

We have only touched on the Kriegsmarine's light cruiser forces in very general terms so far. The German Navy was allowed to retain light units after the Treaty of Versailles in 1919. When new construction began again in the 1920s, the only design available was the World War 1 style of eight 15 cm guns with little anti-aircraft protection. The *Emden,* which was launched in January 1925, suffered badly from that defect and was relegated to a minelaying role in the Baltic and Norwegian waters, where she also carried out an occasional training task. She was attacked several times and eventually she was scuttled after repeated RAF attacks at Kiel in April 1945. Perhaps her greatest claim to fame was her part in the 1945 evacuation of East Prussia already mentioned.

The *Emden* design led to the construction of a three-unit class of light cruisers named after German industrial cities: *Karlsruhe, Köln* and *Königsberg.* This class was designed with commerce raiding in mind and their range was intended to allow them to operate in distant Atlantic waters. Their aircraft, which would have proved very useful throughout their careers, were removed to save weight during half-life refits. *Karlsruhe's* war service did not last long. Under the command of Kapitän zur See Rieve, she was leading the attack on Kristiansand and Arendal when, on April 10 1940, HMS/M *Truant* so badly damaged her with torpedoes that she was abandoned and the torpedo-boat *Greif* had to finish her off. The Germans had lost three capital ships in two days: *Blücher, Karlsruhe* and *Königsberg.*

The second unit of the class, *Königsberg,* was also engaged in the Norwegian campaign of 1940 and was allocated to the Bergen attack group with the *Köln.* On April 10, *Königsberg* was attacked by 15 Skua dive-bombers and she later sank as a result. She was raised in 1943 but capsized in September 1944 and was abandoned. *Köln* was somewhat luckier, starting her war service during the attack on Poland with *Nürnberg* and *Leipzig* under Vize-Admiral Duesch, moving to the North Sea from October to December 1939. After the capture of Bergen, the *Köln* moved to the Baltic in 1941 to prevent a possible break-out by the Soviet Baltic Fleet. In the Baltic she was unsuccessfully attacked by the Soviet *Shch-323* off Sweden, but on April 30 1945 the USAAF struck at Wilhelmshaven and *Köln* finished her career on the bottom of the basin.

As a result of the experience gained with the K-Class, the *Leipzig,* launched in 1929, had a broader beam and more powerful engines installed. Most of her war service was spent in the sea areas where the German capital ships had not inconsiderable success—the Arctic and the Baltic. Her 15 cm guns were to prove a useful addition to the artillery of the ground forces struggling on the Eastern Front. The Polish campaign saw Vize-Admiral Deusch's light cruiser force bombarding sea forts before moving into the North Sea from September to December 1939, when on the 13th HMS/M *Salmon* torpedoed *Leipzig* and *Nürnberg,* the latter then having to put in for repairs. In 1941, Käpitan zur See Stickling took the cruiser to the Baltic and was nearly sunk by *Shch–317,* a Soviet submarine. Later in the war, the ship became a Korvetten-Kapitän's command when she was made ready for a desperate attempt to stem the flood of the Red Army. She survived the war only to be scuttled off Lister on July 20 1946.

Modified from the preceding light cruisers, the *Nürnberg* was another unit which served in northern seas. Launched in 1934, she was active in Polish waters and in the North Sea minelaying operations. As has already been mentioned, the cruiser was damaged by submarine action. After repair, *Nürnberg* (Kapitän zur See von Studnitz) was used to assist the blockade of Soviet naval forces. In January 1945, the cruiser moved west to mine the Skagerrak despite numerous British air attacks, but her efforts were in vain and, later that year, she surrendered, in Danish waters, with the heavy cruiser *Prinz Eugen.* The *Nürnberg* became, in 1946, the Soviet cruiser *Admiral Makarov.*

Towards the end of the war the German Army was so bottled up on the Eastern (Russian) Front that every effort was made by Gross-Admiral Dönitz (who had replaced Gross-Admiral Raeder in January 1943) to give the Army every support which the surface fleet could render. Hitler had suggested several times to the German Naval Staff (Seekriegsleitung: SKL) that as the capital ships did not seem to be achieving much, their guns and equipment should be landed and used to assist the Army in Russia, Poland and later Prussia.

As we have seen, cruiser units were engaged in the bombardment from the sea in support of the troops, which although it may not have been too pleasant for the inhabitants of the target areas, meant that by May 1944 no Kriegsmarine capital ship was in a position to interfere with a cross-Channel invasion and the opening of a second front.

It must be remembered that *Hipper* had been paid off and the *Tirpitz* along with *Gneisenau* were out of commission. The pre-Dreadnought battleships *Schlesien* and *Schleswig-Holstein,* both launched in 1906, had been reduced to an operational training role by 1939. However, so great was the need for heavy artillery support in the Baltic that they were pressed into service. *Schlesien* was active in Danish waters during the invasion of Norway with *Schleswig-Holstein* deployed to Nyborg and Korson. The former warship was mined in May 1945 and scrapped in 1949 after having been partially salved and berthed at Königsberg in 1947. The latter ended her days at Gdynia after suffering major damage from RAF bombers in late 1944. The auxiliary cruiser (or 'raider') *Atlantis* had the benefit of *Schlesien's* 15 cm main guns when the latter was reduced to harbour service.

We have not dealt fully with the careers of the armoured ships *Admiral Graf Spee* and *Admiral Scheer.* The former was the first capital ship to be lost to the Axis cause, but she did cause a tremendous problem for the British and French Navies in the South Atlantic and Indian Oceans with eight hunting groups being formed to search for her. At the same time *Deutschland* (later *Lützow*) was active north of the equator causing a major headache for the Admiralty. Fortunately for Britain, the Battle of the River Plate led to the demise of *Graf Spee. Deutschland,* now called the *Lützow,* moved to the North Sea and later to Norway, where she stayed for a while moving up and down the coast, although she did attempt to break out into the Atlantic on June 12–13 1941. She was caught by a Beaufort torpedo-bomber and limped back to Germany for dry docking until January 1942. She was again damaged when she ran aground in a Norwegian fjord, but was at Altenfjord in December 1943. Spending her remaining war service in the Arctic and Baltic, *Lützow* was scuttled at Swinemunde only to be raised by the Russians and pressed into service until 1948/9.

In October 1940 *Admiral Scheer* (launched in 1933 and sister-ship to the *Graf Spee*) set out for the Atlantic to raid merchantmen and the *Jervis Bay* episode already mentioned shows that she was not that successful, but the Admiralty did cease convoy operations for a fortnight because of her. The *Scheer* was now in the South Atlantic and the Royal Navy searched in vain for her after she rounded the Cape to the Seychelles. Returning to Norway in March 1941, *Scheer* succeeded in sinking 17 merchantmen—one of the more successful German capital ship operations.

In 1942 she was in Norway and on station for one of the most infamous convoy battles of World War 2—PQ17. It was perhaps the most successful series of events for the German capital ship units because it was their presence, not their action, which resulted in loss of 24 ships from the convoy. When the SKL discovered exactly where PQ17 was they moved the *Tirpitz/Admiral Hipper* squadron up to Altenfjord. Luck was not totally on their side as their three destroyers and the *Lützow* managed to run aground!

The Royal Navy believed that *Tirpitz, Admiral Scheer* and *Admiral Hipper* were at sea and, remembering the *Scharnhorst/Gneisenau* incident in 1941, ordered the convoy to scatter and sent the escorts off to repel the supposed attack. The merchantmen were left to the submarines and aircraft although the capital ship squadron actually turned away and returned to the safety of its fjords—such were the orders from Berlin. It should not be forgotten that the Kriegsmarine was without the luxury, almost necessity, of an effective cruiser screen for its largest units.

It would be easy to summarise the capital ship's part of the German war effort by saying that it was a latent threat to convoy operations, but that would not do justice to the commerce-raider endeavours of the cruisers and armoured ships. Neither would one be acknowledging the herculean effort put into the bombardment of the Baltic coast. Above all, the German seaman was let down by the political ineptitude and indecisive leadership of Berlin. What would have happened in a battle squadron to battle squadron engagement we shall never know, but one thing is certain, the German sailor would not have been found lacking in ability or courage.

ABOUT THE PHOTOGRAPHS

The photographs in this book have been selected with care from the Bundesarchiv, Koblenz (the approximate German equivalent of the US National Archives or the British Public Records Office). Particular attention has been devoted to choosing photographs which will be fresh to the majority of readers, although it is inevitable that one or two may be familiar. Other than this, the author's prime concern has been to choose good-quality photographs which illustrate the type of detail that enthusiasts and modellers require. In certain instances quality has, to a degree, been sacrificed in order to include a particularly interesting photograph. For the most part, however, the quality speaks for itself.

The Bundesarchiv files hold some one million black and white negatives of Wehrmacht and Luftwaffe subjects, including 150,000 on the Kriegsmarine, some 20,000 glass negatives from the inter-war period and several hundred colour photographs. Sheer numbers is one of the problems which makes the compilation of a book such as this difficult. Other difficulties include the fact that, in the vast majority of cases, the negatives have not been printed so the researcher is forced to look through box after box of 35 mm contact strips – some 250 boxes containing an average of over 5,000 pictures each, plus folders containing a further 115,000 contact prints of the Waffen-SS; moreover, cataloguing and indexing the negatives is neither an easy nor a short task, with the result that, at the present time, Luftwaffe and Wehrmacht subjects as well as entirely separate theatres of operations are intermingled in the same files.

There is a simple explanation for this confusion. The Bundesarchiv photographs were taken by war correspondents attached to German military units, and the negatives were originally stored in the Reich Propaganda Ministry in Berlin. Towards the close of World War 2, all the photographs – then numbering some $3\frac{1}{2}$ million – were ordered to be destroyed. One man in the Ministry, a Herr Evers, realised that they should be preserved for posterity and, acting entirely unofficially and on his own initiative, commandeered the first available suitable transport – two refrigerated fish trucks – loaded the negatives into them, and set out for safety. Unfortunately, one of the trucks disappeared en route and, to this day, nobody knows what happened to it. The remainder were captured by the Americans and shipped to Washington, where they remained for 20 years before the majority were returned to the government of West Germany. A large number, however, still reside in Washington. Thus the Bundesarchiv files are incomplete, with infuriating gaps for any researcher. Specifically, they end in the autumn of 1944, after Arnhem, and thus record none of the drama of the closing months of the war.

The photographs are currently housed in a modern office block in Koblenz, overlooking the River Mosel. The priceless negatives are stored in the basement, and there are strict security checks on anyone seeking admission to the Bildarchiv (Photo Archive). Regrettably, and the author has been asked to stress this point, the archives are *only open to bona fide authors and publishers, and prints can only be supplied for reproduction in a book or magazine.* They CANNOT be supplied to private collectors or enthusiasts for personal use, so *please* – don't write to the Bundesarchiv or the publishers of this book asking for copy prints, because they cannot be provided. The well-equipped photo laboratory at the Bundesarchiv is only capable of handling some 80 to 100 prints per day because each is printed individually under strictly controlled conditions – another reason for the fine quality of the photographs but also a contributory factor in the above legislation.

Right *Bismarck* rests in dry dock for a final inspection of her underwater hull before beginning her shakedown cruise (B29/2/32).

THE PHOTOGRAPHS

Left A naval assault company is landed near Westerplatte on September 1 1939. Although repulsed at first, the company, landed from the *Schleswig-Holstein*, took the town on September 7 (MN/757/5a).

Below left *Schleswig-Holstein* lies off the Polish coast together with a *Vorpostenboot* (VP-boat) which has definite trawler ancestry (MN/1002/7a).

Right *Schleswig-Holstein* was used during the German attack and occupation of Nyborg and Korson (MN/1001/19).

Below The angular superstructure of the old battleship shows up well in this sunlit scene (MN/1001/20).

Left The after turreted 28 cm guns of the *Schleswig-Holstein* with the two after 9 cm mountings on the superstructure (MN/1595/20a).

Below left The jutting pre-Dreadnought style stem of *Schleswig-Holstein* screens the after superstructure of *Schlesien* (MN/1585/1a).

Below The foremast tower structure of one of the pre-Dreadnought battleships is very reminiscent of Jutland, a battle in which one of the class was sunk (MN/680/23).

Right The Captain of *Schleswig-Holstein* addresses the amassed crew. The trunked together two forward funnels and long pole masts give her a somewhat top heavy look (MN/1571/22a).

Below right The *Schlesien* and *Schleswig-Holstein* were both used in the Baltic with some success as seaward artillery support for the Army (MO/680/35).

Above *Bismarck* seen during the final phase of fitting out in 1940. Some idea of the battleship's size can be gauged from this shot (B1/1/7a).

Left *Schleswig-Holstein* negotiates the Baltic ice in the winter of 1939/40 (86MW/4268/20).

Below left Fairlead and jackstay detail – note the wooden planking. A good picture for super detail modellers (B2/1/15).

Below right The starboard boat-deck and bridge wing of *Schleswig-Holstein* as she pushes on towards her destination – perhaps the North Sea (MO14/683/33a).

Above Surprisingly perhaps, *Bismarck* was equipped for minesweeping as this neatly stowed paravane shows (B2/4/39).

Below The boat decks and aircraft catapult in this shot show just how cramped the amidships area was and yet the equipment was said to operate well in action (B3/1/10).

Above *Bismarck* ran her trials in the Baltic in early 1941 before setting off on Operation Rheinübung in May of that year (B3/5/16).

Below a very clear view of the forward 38 cm guns – weapons that later sunk the *Hood*, the pride of the Royal Navy (B5/2/7).

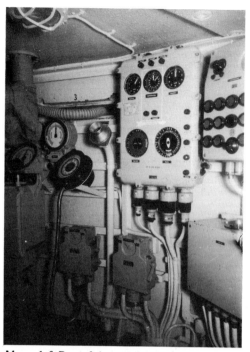 

Above left Part of the control room gear. The various gauges include a ship's head indicator, a log and clock. A gyro compass repeater is also visible (B5/6/39).

Above right The mainmast with its complex radio aerial array. It was chatter on this radio that led to the *Bismarck*'s downfall (B7/7/10).

Below The directors were clustered around the single large funnel – note the gearing mechanism below (B19/2/32).

Above One of *Bismarck*'s pulling whalers or cutters – a maid of all work whose duties could include towing the Arado floatplanes (B6/6/24).

Below Secondary and tertiary armament – the dual purpose 15 cm turret on the main deck and the 10.5 cm AA turret a deck higher (B6/6/26).

Above left Fitting out in Blohm and Voss's Hamburg yard is partially completed and a German newsreel team is there to document the scene (112MW/5562/28a).

Left Work on *Bismarck* seems to have come to a halt in rather severe weather conditions (112MW/5562/25).

Above Fitting out is almost completed in this view of *Bismarck* in the winter of 1940/41. The bridge top director has yet to be fitted (MN/1396/6a).

Right A Kriegsmarine movie-cameraman catches the scene as Admiral Lütjens comes aboard his new flagship and ultimately his deathplace (MN/1403/26a).

Above Mounting the companionway of *Bismarck*, the Fleet Commander is saluted by the assembled ship's company (MN/1361/26a).

Left Kapitän zur See Lindemann greets Günter-Lütjens on *Bismarck*, the pride of the Kriegsmarine until that fateful day – May 27 1941. Lütjens was fresh from the successful cruise with the battlecruiser squadron but found Vice Admiral Tovey more than a match (MN/1362/4a).

Above right and right Getting underway – *Bismarck*'s mooring wires are stowed and the pulling cutter secured (MN/1403/8a and 15a).

Background photograph Unfortunately this is the only photograph of *Tirpitz* which has come to light in the Bundesarchiv. It shows the dazzle painted battleship during a brief foray from the safety of her Norwegian lair (MN/915/23).

Inset left *Scharnhorst* after post-refit trials. The clipper bow and capped funnel are new (MW/269/2a).

Inset above Looking forward along the starboard side with a good view of a secondary 15 cm turret with a camouflaged top (MW/904/21).

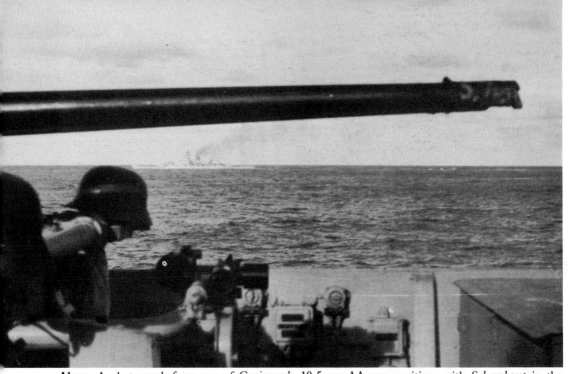

Above A photograph from one of *Gneisenau's* 10.5 cm AA gun positions with *Scharnhorst* in the background. Note the gun crew's helmets are easy to hand if the call to action comes (MW/904/26).

Below A grey day in the North Sea as *Scharnhorst* and *Gneisenau* patrol together during Operation Nordmark in 1940 (MW/905/15).

Above The rather bare quarter deck of *Gneisenau* with *Scharnhorst*'s hull obscured by the waves of a February day (MW/905/34a).

Below The long clipper bows of the battlecruisers meant that they were wet ships even in a moderate sea (MW/906/20a).

Left A good view of the port amidships main deck area. One of the secondary 15 cm gun turrets, of which eight were carried, and a 3.7 cm Flak position are clearly shown (MW/905/4).

Above *Scharnhorst* moving at speed up the Channel during the famous dash from Brest to Germany by Vize-Admiral Cilax's squadron. Note the two German fighters flying top cover (74aMW/3694/22).

Right In close formation, the squadron races on. Cilax's flagship *Scharnhorst* has her guns at the ready quartering the sky. In fact for the 'dash' additional 20 mm guns were mounted on both battlecruisers (74aMW/3695/20).

Left To the right is a 10.5 cm AA gun with its barrels to skyward. On the horizon two destroyers keep company with another capital ship (MW/906/4a).

Below left *Gneisenau* photographed from the conning tower of an escorting U-boat. Submarines frequently operated with German capital ships, especially in the early war years (109MW/5437/8).

Right *Scharnhorst* shares an icy scene with a German tug boat. This battlecruiser served in most operational theatres of the German capital ship effort and was eventually sunk in late 1943 (86MW/4268/16).

Below In the ice floes of the polar seas, the battlecruiser *Gneisenau* lies at anchor. Note the Arado floatplane on its high platform amidships (112MW/5551/2).

Left *Scharnhorst*'s forward mountings – the triple-barrelled 28 cm guns – come in for a spot of maintenance so important to keep them in fighting trim. The warship appears to be making steerage – note the lookout on the starboard side at the eyes of the ship (112MW/5556/16).

Below The ship's company mass on the quarterdeck. The heavily protected gun muzzle and the floatplane catapult gear on the turret roof are noteworthy (112MW/5555/12).

Right The signal platform on the main conning tower of *Scharnhorst*'s superstructure (112MW/5556/22).

Below right *Gneisenau* and *Prinz Eugen* seen from *Scharnhorst*. The gun mounting in the foreground is the very characteristic twin 10.5 cm AA turret (112MW/5555/20).

Above left The Arado reconnaissance plane of the battlecruiser *Scharnhorst* is hoisted aboard after a successful sortie. These aircraft were worth their weight in gold before the advent of surface warning radar (112MW/5558/21).

Left This Arado Ar 196A fits snugly into its nook amidships of *Scharnhorst*. The folding wings are characteristic of naval aircraft but the Luftwaffe mechanics looking on show that the Kriegsmarine, like the British Fleet Air Arm between the wars, did not have full control of its naval aviation (112MW/5570/5).

Above An early U-boat moves up harbour after a war cruise past the newly refitted battlecruiser *Scharnhorst* (112MW/5566/20).

Right In the mid-war years *Scharnhorst* could be told apart from her sister-ship *Gneisenau* by the former's independent mainmast illustrated here (112MW/5570/24).

Above Newly joined recruits are shown a plan of the between decks layout of their new home. A 38,900-ton warship takes some time to become familiar to a new seaman, especially on perhaps his first seagoing service (112MW/5570/16).

Below *Scharnhorst*'s band – a very popular institution on board – practise on the quarterdeck (112MW/5570/19).

Above The Kriegsmarine was as houseproud as any other navy! Note the Type 1934 destroyer in the upper left of this picture (112MW/5570/34).

Below A blurred shot of deck swabbing using a fire hose – perhaps the photographer was the subject of some ho(r)seplay? (112MW/5570/38).

Above left Shssh! This cartoon seems to be a sort of 'walls have ears' notice – perhaps during the preparations for Operation Cerberus, which was after all planned at Brest, an occupied port (112MW/5558/31).

Above *Scharnhorst*'s main machinery control-room with the engineering Officer of the Watch in the foreground (112MW/5574/12a).

Left Who says that T-shirts sporting motifs are new? Note the plated-over gun position in the foreground (112MW/5580/18a).

Above right These battlecruiser anchors appear to have been just delivered to a German naval port from Stuttgart. The inscription can be loosely translated as 'please leave alone'. (112MW/5589/13a).

Right The Kriegsmarine was very fond of its mascots – this one is from *Gneisenau* (MN/901/36).

Left This photo has been beautifully framed by examples of *Prinz Eugen*'s main and secondary armament. The battlecruiser in the centre is *Scharnhorst* (MW/6071/36a).

Below left The deadly duo move at speed – operating together these two capital ships wreaked havoc in the Atlantic sea-lanes and sank the British aircraft carrier *Glorious* off Norway (MW/6074/29a).

Right A rather exposed searchlight sponson on *Gneisenau*'s funnel. Mind you, the smoke emission cannot have been very popular either (MN/901/27).

Below A battlecruiser's large searchlight – another part of the ship's equipment rendered somewhat obsolete by radar (MN/901/30).

Above Chipping ice from the main forward mountings during operations in the Artic. Ice always presents a problem to ships when it forms on the upper deck causing an increase in top weight (MN/901/20).

Below The forward 28 cm battery of *Scharnhorst* – called Anton – is somewhat frozen and in fact the whole ship has a Christmas cake-like appearance (MN/903/15).

Above The port capstan and icy 'Anton' make a rather picturesque backdrop for this shot for the family album (MN/903/32).

Below 'We see no ships' – perhaps just as well judging by the iced up condition of the main armament (MN/903/34).

Left *Gneisenau*'s main machinery space. The leather jerkins of the stokers are noteworthy (MN/903/38).

Below A chip fryer? This piece of ship's machinery is so far unidentified (MN/906/38a).

Right A good shot for those modellers who like to superdetail – *Gneisenau*'s starboard side (MN/904/25).

Below right 10.5 cm Flak gun crews were exercised regularly. One such crew is seen here loading shells into the breech (MN/907/23).

Above left A communications number keeps watch as *Gneisenau* moves north along the Norwegian coast. Note the large German destroyer in the background (MN/1623/29a).

Above Clearing ice from *Scheer*'s quarterdeck. The weather was at times the worst enemy of the Kriegsmarine, especially in Arctic waters (111MW/5543/27a).

Left *Admiral Scheer* off Norway taken from a rather frosty *Prinz Eugen*. A day or so after this photograph was probably taken, *Eugen* was damaged by the British submarine *Trident* off Trondheim (MW/6077/18a).

Above right A view of *Scheer*'s superstructure taken from the fo'c's'le. Note the large searchlights on their sponsons midway up the conning tower (111MW/5543/16a).

Right This view from the quarter deck was taken between the two banks of 55 cm torpedo tubes (111MW/5543/24a).

Background photograph In June 1941 the armoured ship *Lützow* (*ex-Deutchsland*) attempted to break out to the Atlantic Ocean but was stopped by the torpedoes of RAF Beaufort aircraft (MN/1025/16a).

Inset A *VP-boat* comes alongside *Lützow* as she lies disabled off Lindesnes. She managed to make the safety of Kiel two days later but was out of the war for seven months (MN/1025/14a).

Above An unusual view – *Hipper* in dry-dock, probably at Brest before an Atlantic raiding voyage in early 1941 (MN/1401/9a).

Left *Hipper* at Cuxhaven with German mountain troops aboard. Note the Arado float-plane on the catapult amidships (113MW/5604/6a).

Right A view from *Admiral Hipper*'s superstructure showing the forward 20 cm batteries. Note the single light anti-aircraft gun on 'B' turret which would seem to date this photograph as early 1940 (113MW/5607/45).

Left An Arado is lowered on to its catapult bogie by the heavy duty seaplane crane on *Hipper* (MW/6081/16a).

Below The catapult is swung into wind and the Arado's Luftwaffe pilot opens up the 970 hp BMW engine. However, the Kriegsmarine observer does not seem to be aboard (MW/1949/2a).

Right One of the capital ship's rangefinders is checked out after her dash from Brest in March 1941 (MW/2296/7a).

Below right Gun cleaning as *Hipper* works up from Brest prior to her second Atlantic foray in February 1941. Note the fresh dazzle paint (MW/1948/20a).

Left This photograph is thought to show Kapitän zur See Meisel chatting to one of his Korvettenkapitän heads of department prior to the *Hipper*'s departure from Brest on February 1 1941 (MW/1948/38a).

Below *Hipper* is prepared for sea at Brest but just what operation or evolution is being carried out on the main deck is uncertain (MW/1947/2).

Right A movie film is shot as the fo'c's'le party puts its house in order. The vessel in front is presumably a pilot to assist in the navigation of restricted waters and swept channels (MW/2242/28a).

Below right *Admiral Hipper* heads out into the Atlantic swell. Note the 20 mm AA gun on the second turret is well shrouded against the elements (MW/1946/31a).

Above left This shot of the mainmast and the mizzen shows the 14 kill pennants displayed by the *Hipper* on her return from a raiding operation in the Atlantic (MW/1948/31a).

Above right A batman gives tender loving care to a Leutnant zur See's jacket (MW/2244/14a).

Below A fine view of a leading seaman adjusting the *Hipper*'s Flak rangefinder gear whilst the heavy cruiser was sailing in northern waters in 1941 (MW/2296/21a).

Above A group of junior officers and a Kapitän-leutnant (second left) relax on the quarter deck of *Admiral Hipper* with their American 78s and record player. The date is probably early 1941 and so US products were probably still obtainable (MW/2299/14a).

Below Naval personnel and dockyard workers look somewhat stonefaced as they await the *Hipper*'s return from operations (MW/2244/31a).

Above It seems from the photograph collection in the Bundesarchiv that German matelots spent much of their time swabbing the decks – in this case it is *Hipper*'s quarterdeck which is having the benefit of a good scrub (MW/2242/5a).

Below Fo'c's'le detail of *Hipper* taken as she moves up fjord to Trondheim. Note the protective muffles for the 20 cm gun barrels (113MW/5604/35a).

Above *Hipper* lands German occupation forces at Trondheim in April 1940 – Operation Weserübung (113MW/5607/31a).

Below *Admiral Hipper* alongside an exposed wharf. This is a particularly good shot for modellers building a diorama. The Hamburg-Amerika Line gangways are especially noteworthy (113MW/5607/4a).

Background photograph In a North Sea storm the RN destroyer *Glowworm* lost contact with the battlecruiser *Renown* only to encounter the *Admiral Hipper*'s squadron. Lieutenant Commander Roofe, RN, succeeded in ramming the *Hipper* before the *Glowworm* was overwhelmed. It was one of the most gallant destroyer actions of the war (757/32/6).

Inset left and following page These grim scenes tell their own story – the bitter North Sea is no place to be, even in April. Soaked with fuel oil, the *Glowworm*'s survivors are hauled aboard the *Hipper* (757/33/26a and 31a).

Inset below A heavy sea breaks over *Hipper*'s bow as her main armament trains to port (MW/1945/21a).

Above The very important chore of swabbing out the gun barrels of the main armament took some effort but was necessary if the weapons were to function correctly during the next shoot. That shoot could involve the ship's safety (MW/1948/19a).

Right To facilitate easy recognition from the air, large red, white and black Nazi emblems were painted on prominent parts of many German capital ships. Here the *Hipper*'s anchor chains are also included in the scheme – but just where the painter is going next could be a problem (MW/2299/5a).

Above left A torpedo boat leads *Gneisenau*, a destroyer, another torpedo boat and *Prinz Eugen* during the famed 'Channel Dash' of February 1942 (74aMW/3695/13).

Left This is probably the heavy cruiser *Blücher*; a photograph taken before her fateful, and final, run to Oslo in April 1940 (MN/1536/32a).

Above Divisions on the quarterdeck of a Kriegsmarine heavy cruiser, possibly the *Blücher* (MN/1003/3a).

Right An unidentified Kapitän zur See (possibly Woldag of the *Blücher*) walks the upper deck. The light cruiser moored behind is probably the *Emden* (MN/1400/10a).

Above left This Luftwaffe floatplane mechanic is catching up with some light reading in a hammock slung from the catapult of his charge (MW/6099/19).

Above right A torn Kriegsmarine ensign bears witness to a rough time at sea during the 'Channel Dash' (MW/6068/15).

Below General Admiral Bachmann greets the members of the *Prinz Eugen*'s ship's company whilst the cruiser was in Brest preparing for Operation Cerberus (113MW/6061/26a).

Above A good shot of *Eugen's* port beam rangefinder gear during a practice shoot in the Biscay area (113MW/6066/35).

Below Detail of the port bridge wing of *Eugen*. Kapitän zur See Brickmann is second from the right (MW/6074/32a).

Background photograph One of the mercantile victims of *Hipper*'s Atlantic raiding cruises. The short range of this action suggests that the *Hipper* is going by the 'Prize' rules of commerce raiding (MW/1946/18a).

Inset left *Eugen*'s guns are tested during a shakedown cruise in the relatively safe waters of the Bay of Biscay. Note the wire gauze of the spent shell catcher for an AA gun, on the left (113MW/6066/33).

Inset right One of *Prinz Eugen*'s 20 mm anti-aircraft guns during a practice shoot. The life-jacket oversmocks are noteworthy (MW/2260/4).

Left A practice session at the breech of one of the *Eugen*'s 10.5 cm anti-aircraft guns. The crew on the left seem to have too many hands! (MW/6091/15a).

Right Spent shell cases are cleared away from the upper deck. These brass items were collected after use and returned to the ammunition factories of the Reich for possible re-use (MW/6075/23a).

Below An intriguing shot of a member of one of *Prinz Eugen*'s turret crew members – more like the Panzers than the Kriegsmarine (MW/6074/30a).

Far left With minesweeper and torpedo boat escort, *Prinz Eugen* heads out into the grey Atlantic – note the Flak-vierling on 'A' turret (113MW/6066/38).

Left *Eugen* at sea with destroyer, torpedo boat and minesweeper escorts. This is probably a scene during the 'Channel Dash' when the 'sweeper escort' was very necessary – even then both battlecruisers involved hit mines before reaching Germany (113MW/6066/26).

Below left One of the paired sets of 53 cm torpedo tubes of the early light cruiser *Emden* receives attention as the ship heads for Oslofjord in April 1940 (M014/676/28).

Right The yeoman (with the binoculars) reads off a message to his subordinates in this view of *Emden*'s signal platform (MN/759/21).

Below Kapitän zur See Lange addresses the ship's company of *Emden* off Norway in 1940. Note the lifebuoy sentry who still remembers his first duty (14MO/680/14).

Left *Emden*'s crew scrub any vestige of battle from their deck after operations in support of the German occupation of Norway. This was one of the few actions in which the old cruiser was employed (MO/681/8a).

Below The cruiser suffered casualties as she forced her way up Oslofjord and here they are being brought ashore for treatment (MO/681/5a).

Right Amongst those casualties there seem to have been four fatalities and here they are awaiting the traditional naval burial at sea. Note also the flag stretched out for identification of nationality from the air (14MO/681/30a).

Below right *Emden* takes on stores off a Baltic port. The 8.8 cm AA gun (left) can be compared for size with the 15 cm mounting in this view (MN/757/16a).

Emden's builders did not equip her adequately for air defence, but her short-range armament was supplemented during the first weeks of hostilities by 20 mm Flakvierlings (14MO/676/13).

Above Oslo forms the backdrop for this picture of the light cruiser *Emden* (14MO/681/24a).

Below Although launched in 1925, this old cruiser could turn on a speed of 25 knots at a push. Note the minelaying gear on the quarterdeck. It was in this role that *Emden* spent most of her war service (MN/1025/6).

Above left One for the folks back home in the Fatherland! Fritz-tar astride a 15 cm mounting on the *Emden* (109MW/5423/28a).

Above right A fine shot of the forward funnel, superstructure and foremast details of the *Emden*, an early light cruiser design (MN/757/10a).

Below A blurred shot of *Karlsruhe* off Norway in April 1940. Her war service was cut short soon after this photograph was taken, when HMS/M *Truant* torpedoed her off the coast (MN/1611/26a).

Above Kapitän zur See Rieve descends to the aftercastle of *Karlsruhe*. Note the ceremonial dagger at his side (MN/1611/13a).

Below A frantic fo'c's'le scene as the *Nürnberg* lies off the Norwegian coast in the autumn of 1940 – probably September (MN/1403/32a).

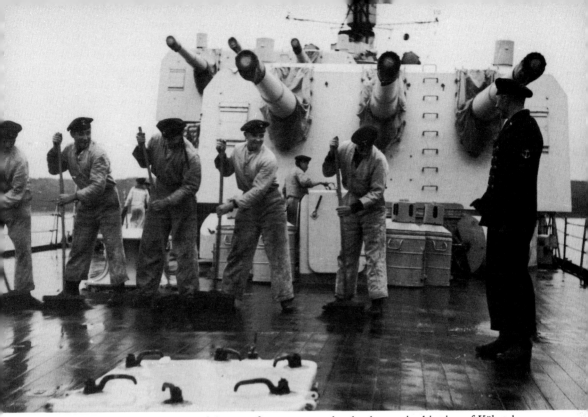

Above The staggered arrangement of the two after turrets can be clearly seen in this view of *Köln* taken from the quarterdeck (109MW/5421/21a).

Below Because the *Köln* is stuck in the ice, a semi-permanent and flagged pathway has been made to the shore. This shot was probably taken in the Baltic where the Kriegsmarine was rarely troubled by the Soviet Air Force (MN/923/25a).

Left This light cruiser design was definitely planned so that the *Nürnberg*'s 32 knots could speed her out of trouble. The forward main battery shown here consisted of three 15 cm guns, whilst the after battery numbered six guns! (MN/1405/6a).

Right Alongside at a Norwegian port, the PT instructor has a group of sailors on the quayside to exercise in the autumn sun (MN/1402/19a).

Below Iced up in the Baltic, *Leipzig* lies off-shore. She spent her latter war service bombarding the ever advancing hordes of the Red Army (92MW/4842/6).

Background photograph A beautiful dawn view of *Nürnberg* anchored off the Norwegian coast. This light cruiser became the *Admiral Makarov* of the Soviet Navy after the war (MN/1405/33a).
Inset *Nürnberg*'s ship's company is called to order by a bugler and the Officer of the Day. Note the 8.8 cm anti-aircraft mounting in the background (MN/1405/29a).

Above As in every navy, a pusser ship is a good ship. This centre-line shot shows the after turrets of *Nürnberg* and the swastika emblem on the deck. The two liners behind are most interesting but are unfortunately unidentified. Any ideas? (MN/1400/31a).

Below A tranquil scene in the Baltic. The sailing vessel looks so out of place beneath a capital ship's guns (MN/1402/10a).

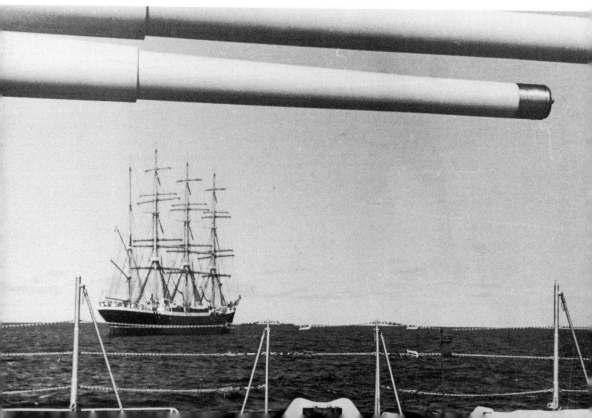

Above On the 'footplate' of a heavy cruiser, although this must surely be another of the posed photographs for consumption at home (MN/907/11).

Below Traditional German maritime entertainment, this picture also shows the standard working dress of the Kriegsmarine sailor (MN/909/31).

APPENDIX

The following is a comprehensive list of German capital ships which served in the Kriegsmarine during World War 2. It does not include the planned and in some cases partially built projects which, for one reason or another, did not come to fruition.
* indicates warship not completed

	Name	Launch Date	Eventual fate
Battleships			
	Schlesien	May 28 1906	Scrapped 1949
	Schleswig-Holstein	Dec 17 1906	Scuttled 1945
	Bismarck	Feb 14 1939	Sunk May 1941
	Tirpitz	Apr 1 1939	Scrapped 1948
Battlecruisers			
	Scharnhorst	Oct 3 1936	Sunk Dec 1943
	Gneisenau	Dec 8 1936	Scrapped 1951
Armoured Ships			
	Deutschland/Lützow	May 19 1931	Scrapped 1948/9
	Admiral Scheer	Apr 1 1933	Bombed 1945
	Admiral Graf Spee	Jun 30 1934	Scuttled 1939
Heavy Cruisers			
	Admiral Hipper	Feb 6 1937	Scuttled 1945
	Blücher	Jun 8 1937	Sunk Apr 1940
	Lützow*	Jul 1 1939	Scrapped 1950
	Prinz Eugen	Aug 22 1938	Sunk USN 1947
	Seydlitz*	Jan 1 1939	Abandoned 1950
Light Cruisers			
	Emden	Jan 7 1925	Scrapped 1947
	Karlsruhe	Aug 20 1927	Sunk Apr 1940
	Köln	May 23 1928	Scrapped 1946
	Königsberg	Mar 26 1927	Sunk Apr 1940
	Leipzig	Oct 18 1929	Scuttled 1946
	Nürnberg	Dec 8 1934	To Russia 1946

For a complete breakdown of the actual fates of the above German capital ships, the reader should consult one of the standard works on the subject.

Other titles in the same series

No 1 Panzers in the desert
by Bruce Quarrie
No 2 German bombers over England
by Bryan Philpott
No 3 Waffen-SS in Russia
by Bruce Quarrie
No 4 Fighters defending the Reich
by Bryan Philpott
No 5 Panzers in North-West Europe
by Bruce Quarrie
No 6 German fighters over the Med
by Bryan Philpott
No 7 German paratroops in the Med
by Bruce Quarrie
No 8 German bombers over Russia
by Bryan Philpott
No 9 Panzers in Russia 1941–43
by Bruce Quarrie
No 10 German fighters over England
by Bryan Philpott
No 11 U-boats in the Atlantic
by Paul Beaver
No 12 Panzers in Russia 1943–45
by Bruce Quarrie
No 13 German bombers over the Med
by Bryan Philpott

In preparation

No 15 German mountain troops
by Bruce Quarrie
No 16 German fighters over Russia
by Bryan Philpott
No 17 E-boats and coastal craft
by Paul Beaver
No 18 German maritime aircraft
by Bryan Philpott
No 19 Panzers in the Balkans and Italy
by Bruce Quarrie
No 20 German destroyers and escorts
by Paul Beaver